NAME _____

1. did Sid read well? _____

2. One note said, "T_____ the oak tree near the door."

3. Is that what Sid did? _____

4. One note said, "Send a c_____ to Sam's tree farm."

5. What did Sid send to the tree farm? _____

6. Where did Sid call to get a con? _____
       the tree farm   the man
       the jail   after he made trees

7. Who said, "I am really doing a good job"? _____

8. Was Sid doing a good job? _____

9. Sid said, "The boss will be _____ of me."
       pouch   proud   sore   tired

> That girl walks slowly.

1. make a p under the word That.

2. make a line over the word that tells how the girl walks.

3. make a line under the words that tell who walks slowly.

One day Sandy counted dogs at the dog farm. On her way to school, she counted ninety dogs. When she came home from school, she counted ninety-nine dogs. She asked, "Why are there more now?"

a mother dog said, "There are more dogs because I got nine baby dogs today."

1. Who counted the dogs? _____

2. how many dogs did she count on her way to school? _____

3. how many dogs did she count after school? _____

4. how many baby dogs did the mother dog get that day? _____

---

look at the picture on page 121 of your reader.

1. The note says, "_____ the oak tree near the door."

2. Is Sid tapping the tree? _____

3. Is the tree growing in the ground? _____

NAME _____   TAKE-HOME **123** SIDE **1**

1. Did Sid send pine trees or pin trees? _____ trees

2. Did Sid send a cone to the farm or a con to the farm? a _____

3. Did Sid tap the tree or tape the tree? _____ the tree

4. One note said, "Plant seeds on the _____."
        slope   slop   slip   ground

5. Where did Sid plant the seeds? in the sl_____

6. Who was walking with her cane? _____

7. Who got very mad? _____

8. Who was very sad? _____

> A car on the road sounds loud.

1. Make a box around the words that tell where the car is.

2. Circle the word that tells how the car sounds.

3. Make a line over the word road.

Copyright © 1995 SRA Macmillan/McGraw-Hill. All rights reserved.

TAKE-HOME 123 SIDE 2

There once was a kite crook. This crook robbed stores. Then she would jump on her kite and fly away. "Ho, ho," she said. "Nobody can get me when I have my kite."

One day a cop said, "I can stop you." He grabbed a log and tossed it. The log hit the kite. The kite hit the ground. Then the crook fell to the ground. The cop said, "I've got you now."

1. The crook had a _____ .

2. Who said, "Nobody can get me when I have my kite"? _____

3. Who said, "I can stop you"? _____

4. What did the cop toss at the kite? _____
      a cop   a dog   a log

Look at the picture on page 124 of your reader.

1. What is Sid planting? _____

2. The note says, "Plant seeds _____ _____ _____ ."

3. What is the name of the plant shop? _____ _____ _____

NAME _____

TAKE-HOME **124** SIDE **1**

1. Who dropped her cane into the can? _____

2. Did Sid plant seeds in
   the slop or on the slope? _____

3. Did he send out pin trees or pine trees? _____ trees

4. Did Sid make a pan or a pane for the window? _____

5. Did Sid send a cone to the
   farm or a con to the farm? _____

6. Did Sid tap the oak tree or tape that tree? _____ the tree

7. Who was very, very sad? _____

> The big boy felt sad.

1. Make a <u>d</u> over the word <u>big</u>.

2. Circle the words that tell who felt sad.

3. Make a line under the word that tells how the big boy felt.

Jane liked to make big things. Once she made a hat for her brother, Walter. That hat was so big that it fell over his ears. It fell over his nose. It came down to his feet.

He said, "I will fix this hat." He cut three holes in it. One hole was for his head. Two holes were for his arms. He said, "This hat is not a good hat. But it is a good coat."

1. Who made the hat? _____

2. Who had the hat on? _____

3. Why didn't the hat sit on his head? _____

4. How many holes did he cut in the hat? _____

5. He said, "It is a good _____ ."

Look at the picture on page 127 of your reader.

1. Does the boss look happy or mad? _____

2. What is on the window? _____

3. What is the boss holding? _____

NAME _____   TAKE-HOME **125** SIDE 1

1. Who said, "I don't read very well"? _____
2. Who said, "I will teach you how to read"? _____
3. Did Sid read well when a week went by? _____
4. One note said, "Tape a cap to my _____ ."
5. Did these notes fool Sid? _____
6. Can Sid read the notes now? _____
7. Does Sid feel happy or sad? _____

> That cow on the road ran fast.

1. Make a box around the words that tell where the cow is.
2. Make an e under the word That.
3. Make a line over the word that tells how the cow ran.

TAKE-HOME 125 SIDE 2

The boss had a cane can. One day, Sid took the cane can. When the boss came back to the shop, she was mad. "I left the cane can here," she said. "But now it is not here. Where is it?"

Sid said, "I planted a tree in the cane can."

So now the cane can is not a cane can. It is a tree pot.

1. Who took the cane can? _____

2. Who got mad? _____

3. What did Sid plant in the cane can? _____

4. Now the cane can is a tree _____ .

Look at the picture on page 130 of your reader.

1. Do you see a pan on the window? _____

2. Is Sid reading? _____

NAME _____   TAKE-HOME **126** SIDE 1

1. The tiger was _____ .
       lame   old   tame   time

2. Did he bite children? _____

3. What did he like to eat? _____
       ice   ice bits   ice cream   ice skates

4. Did the tiger have any cash? _____

5. What was in his pouch? _____
       stops   cones   stones   rocks

6. Did the man like the stones? _____

7. Who said, "What will you do with a big cone and some string"? _____

8. Who said, "Wait and see"? _____

9. The tiger made the cone into a h_____ .

> The boy felt cold in the rain.

1. Make a box around the word that tells how the boy felt.

2. Make a box around the words that tell where the boy is.

3. Make a line over the words that tell who felt cold.

One day, the boss left a note for Sid. Here is what that note said: "Tape my cane with a bit of white tape. The white tape is in the tape can."

Do you think Sid did what the note said? Yes, he did. After he looked at the note, he got the white tape and taped the cane.

1. Who left the note for Sid? _____

2. The note told Sid to _____ a cane.

3. Where was the white tape? _____
    in the tap can   in the tape can

4. Sid got the tape and taped the _____ .

| All the big horses are tired. |

Circle every horse that is tired.

NAME _____   TAKE-HOME **127** SIDE 1

1. How many ghosts lived in the old house? _____

2. How many ghosts were mean? _____

3. Boo was not a _____ ghost.
        old   mean   big   fat

4. What did Boo like to do? _____
        make everybody happy   make people mad
        act mean   scare farmers

5. Were the people in town afraid of Boo? _____

6. Were the other ghosts he lived with afraid of Boo? _____

7. What is the title of this story? _____

★★★

1. Did Sid tap the oak tree or tape the oak tree?

    _____ the oak tree

2. Who told Sid, "I will teach you to read"?

    _____

3. Did Sid become good at reading? _____

> Six cats sat in a tree.

1. Make a line under the words that tell where the cats were.

2. Circle the words that tell who sat in the tree.

3. Make an <u>s</u> over the word <u>sat</u>.

One day Spot was walking down the street in her big yellow wig. A wind came up and her wig went flying into the sky. An eagle was flying near Spot. This eagle was a bald eagle. The wig landed on her head. Then the eagle said, "Now I am not a bald eagle. I am a yellow eagle."

1. Spot had on her big _____ _____.
2. What made the wig fly away? _____
    the sun   the moon   the wind
3. Who got the wig? _____
4. Is the eagle bald now? _____

> Every big fish eats plants.

Circle every fish that eats plants.

NAME _____   TAKE-HOME **128** SIDE 1

1. What is the title of this story?
   _____

2. Who was sitting in his seat, reading a book? _____

3. Which ghost said, "We don't care where you go"?
   _____

      the smallest ghost   the oldest ghost
         the biggest ghost   the fastest ghost

4. Who did Boo see crying near the stream? _____

5. What did the frog say he really was? a _____
       monster   king   queen   ghost

6. Did the frog think that Boo could help him? _____

★★★

1. What did the tame tiger like to eat? _____

2. Did the tame tiger give the man cash or stones? _____

3. The tiger made the cone into a _____ .

> A fish jumped in the water.

1. Circle the words that tell who jumped.
2. Make a box around the words that tell where the fish jumped.
3. Make a <u>v</u> over the word <u>jumped</u>.

Copyright © 1995 SRA Macmillan/McGraw-Hill. All rights reserved.

One day the con fox said, "I need a good meal." So he went to a hot dog stand. Then he began to sing and sing. He did not sing well.

The man said, "Get out of here."

But the con fox did not stop. At last, the man got so mad that he began to throw hot dogs at the fox. The fox said, "Thank you. I need a good meal."

1. The fox said, "I need a good _____."

2. So he went to a _____ _____ stand.

3. Who began to sing? _____

4. Why did the man tell the fox to go away?

   The fox _____

5. What did the man throw at the fox? _____

Jane has all the big kites.

Circle every kite that Jane has.

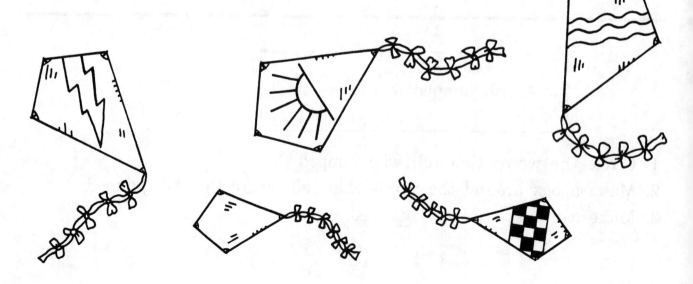

NAME _____   TAKE-HOME **129** SIDE 1

1. Who said, "I will help you"? _____

2. Who said, "The monster is in my castle"? _____

3. Boo floated over the _____ .
       town   lake   sky   moon

4. When Boo floated near the castle, the _____ began to howl.
       ghosts   hounds   cows   monster

5. Who said, "I'll turn you into a frog or a toad"? the _____
       king   ghost   monster   hound

6. The monster was holding a gold _____ .
       hat   mouse   rod   toad

7. Who said, "I must get that magic rod from the monster"? _____

8. What is the title of this story? _____

★★★

1. Who worked for the boss? _____

2. Did Sid send a cone to the farm or a con to the farm? a _____

3. Did the note tell Sid to plant seeds on the slope or in the slop? _____

> The snow on the hill looks white.

1. Make an r over the word snow.
2. Circle the word white.
3. Make a box around the words that tell where the snow is.

Copyright © 1995 SRA Macmillan/McGraw-Hill. All rights reserved.

There was an elephant that liked to jump. Everybody tried to get him to stop jumping. He was making a mess. One day a tiger said, "I will stop his jumping." The tiger made a big hole in the ground. She put grass over the hole. Then she told the elephant to jump on that grass. When the elephant jumped, he fell into the hole. Fifty bugs tickled him and tickled him. The elephant said he would not jump again. Now everybody is happy.

1. Who liked to jump? _____

2. The tiger made a h_____ in the ground.

3. Fifty _____ tickled the elephant.

| Pam has all of the little kites. |

Circle every kite that Pam has.

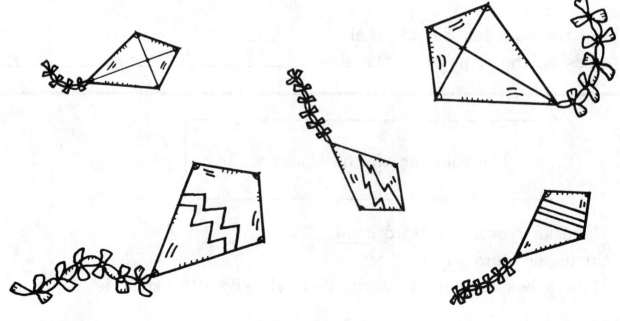

NAME _____   TAKE-HOME **130** SIDE **1**

1. Boo wanted to get the magic _____ from the monster.

2. Who tried to scare the monster? _____

3. Was the monster scared? _____

4. Did the monster laugh? _____

5. What did Boo have growing from his back? a big _____
      fan   fun   fat   fin

6. Who was really scared? _____

7. Boo was part _____ and part ghost.
      frog   fig   fish   fear

8. Did Boo think of a plan? _____

★★

| Fill in the blanks. |

1. How many mean ghosts lived with Boo? _____

2. The monster had made the king into a _____ .

3. The monster had a gold _____ .

> The rock feels hard in my hand.

1. Circle the words that tell what feels hard.
2. Circle the word that tells how the rock feels.
3. Make a line over the words that tell where the rock is.

One day a car stopped near Spot. A dog and a cow were in that car. Spot said, "Who are you?"

The dog said, "Bark."

Spot said, "So your name is Mark. Where are you going, Mark?"

The cow said, "Moooooo."

Spot said, "So you are going to the zoo. I hope you have fun."

1. What stopped near Spot? _____

2. Who was in that car? a _____ and a _____

3. What did Spot think the dog said? _____

4. What did Spot think the cow said? _____

Sandy counted all of the little balls.

Circle every ball that Sandy counted.

NAME _____   TAKE-HOME **131** SIDE **1**

1. What is the title of this story? _____

2. Boo had a plan for getting the gold _____ from the monster.

3. Who said, "I found somebody you can't scare"? _____

4. How many ghosts jumped up from the table? _____

5. Which ghost made himself as big as a horse?

   the _____

       gold house   biggest ghost
       oldest ghost   smallest ghost

6. What did the five ghosts do when they saw Boo's fins and tail?

   They started to _____ .
       laugh   cry   think   get scared

7. Were the five ghosts afraid to go to the monster's castle? _____

★★

1. Who told Sid, "I will teach you to read"? _____

2. Did Sid become good at reading? _____

3. Does Sid feel happy or sad? _____

> The monster held a gold rod over the toad.

1. Make a <u>b</u> over the word <u>held</u>.
2. Make a box around the words that tell who held a gold rod.
3. Circle the words that tell where he held the gold rod.

Every day a mean bird would scare people in town. That bird said, "It is fun to scare people. So I'll scare them at night." So the bird began to play tricks on people at night. Then one night a man shouted at the bird. The bird got scared. Now the bird does not scare people any more.

1. This story is about a mean _____ .

2. What did that bird like to do? _____ people

3. Who shouted at the bird? _____

| Sam made all of the little dresses. |

Circle every dress that Sam made.

NAME _____   TAKE-HOME **132** SIDE **1**

1. What is the title of this story? _____

2. Who began to howl when the ghosts got near the castle? the _____
      mouse   house   hounds   horse

3. Did one of the ghosts scare the hounds? _____

4. Who was sitting at the table when the ghosts floated in? _____

5. What broke into a thousand pieces? _____

6. Who said, "I'm leaving"? _____

7. Did Boo pick up the magic rod? _____

8. Who grabbed the magic rod? the _____
     old hound   monster   Boo   biggest ghost

★★

1. The woman told Don to do _____ things.

2. The woman handed Don a _____ .

3. Don _____ the dime to his _____ .

> The castle was on the hill.

1. Make a line under the words that tell what was on the hill.
2. Circle the word <u>was</u>.
3. Make a line over the words that tell where the castle was.

TAKE-HOME 132 SIDE 2

One day the con fox said, "I will get some cash from a store. I will get a fish pole. I will drop a line down to the cash box and steal some cash."

So the con fox got on top of the store. He dropped his line down into the store. Then he lifted it as hard as he could. But he didn't have a cash box on the end of his line. He had a big cop on the end of his line. Now the con fox is in jail. He is a con.

1. Who said, "I will get cash from a store"? _____

2. What did he get? a _____

3. Was a fish on his line? _____

4. What was on his line? _____

5. Where is the con fox now? _____

| Every elephant is in the zoo. |

Circle every animal that is in the zoo.

NAME _____   TAKE-HOME **133** SIDE **1**

1. What is the title of this story? _____

2. Did the biggest ghost try to turn Boo into a leaf? _____

3. Did the biggest ghost turn Boo into a leaf? _____

4. Who said, "This thing doesn't work"? _____

5. The biggest ghost said, "Bine bin, f_____ f_____."

6. Did the biggest ghost turn into a big yellow flower? _____

7. Were the other ghosts sad when one ghost turned into a leaf? _____

8. Were there words on the side of the rod? _____

9. Did the ghost read these words? _____

10. The ghost holding the rod said, "I can't _____."

★★

1. Could Don run fast when he was a super man? _____

2. Who made a hole in the school? _____

3. Did the boys and girls like Don or hate him? _____

> That red truck was outside.

1. Make a box around the words that tell what was outside.
2. Make a line under the word that tells where the red truck was.
3. Make a c over the word was.

A monster named Ib had the biggest teeth you have seen. He would show his teeth to people and they would scream. Then they would run away. One day Ib showed his teeth to a little girl. But she didn't scream and run away. She said, "Your teeth are yellow. They need a good brushing." She took out her tooth brush and brushed the monster's teeth. Now the monster is happy. He has white teeth.

1. What was the monster's name? _____

2. Ib had big _____ .

3. Did the little girl run away? _____

4. What did she do to the monster's teeth? _____
       hit them   sat on them   brushed them

5. Why is the monster happy now? _____

| Linda picked every big flower. |

Circle all the flowers that Linda picked.

NAME _____

TAKE-HOME **134** SIDE **1**

1. How many ghosts could read the words? _____

2. Which ghost could read the words? _____

3. Boo said, "Bit bite, ben _____ ."

4. Did the ghosts feel mean then? _____

5. Did a ghost feel like helping a farmer? _____

6. Did Boo turn the flower into a monster or a ghost? _____

7. Who said magic words to make Boo's tail go away? _____

★★

1. Who worked for the boss? _____

2. Did Sid send a cone to the farm or a con to the farm? _____

3. Did the note tell Sid to plant seeds in the slop or on the slope?
   _____

> A green frog scared the ghosts.

1. Circle the words that tell who scared the ghosts.

2. Make a line under the word ghosts.

3. Make a line over the word green.

Once there was a very sad snake. That snake could not kick a ball. All the other animals kicked the ball. But snakes do not have legs.

Then one day the snake said, "I will use my head." And she did. Now she can make the ball go as far as the other animals can. But the snake doesn't kick the ball. She hits the ball with her head.

The other animals all say, "That snake can really use her head."

1. Why was the snake sad? She couldn't _____ .

2. Snakes do not have l_____ .

3. Who said, "I will use my head"? _____

4. Can the snake make the ball go far? _____

| If a horse is running, she is old. |

Circle every horse that is old.

NAME _____   TAKE-HOME **135** SIDE **1**

1. Boo had turned the mean ghosts into _____ ghosts.
     sitting   smiling   mean

2. Boo said, "Hog, sog, bumpy _____ ."

3. Who said, "You must come to live with me"? _____

4. Who was shy? _____

5. Did Boo go to live with the king? _____

6. People went out at night to find _____ .
     monsters   farmers   ghosts

★★★

| Fill in the blanks. |

1. How many mean ghosts lived with Boo? _____

2. Which ghost could read the words on the gold rod? _____

3. Are the people in Boo's town afraid of ghosts now? _____

> The girl sat in her tent.

1. Make a box around the words that tell who sat in the tent.

2. Circle the words that tell where the girl sat.

3. Make an r over the word sat.

The con fox said, "It is getting cold out. I need a new coat. So I will go out and con somebody out of a coat." So the con fox went out. He saw some white coats near a farm house. But when he tried to grab those coats, he found out that they were ghosts. So the con fox ran back to his cold house.

1. Who said, "It is getting cold out"? _____

2. What did the con fox want? _____
      a coat   a box   a sheet

3. So he went to a farm _____ .

4. What were the coats? _____
      men   farmers   ghosts

| If a girl is swimming, she is tall. |

Circle every girl who is tall.

NAME _____ TAKE-HOME **136** SIDE 1

1. Who was going to genie school? _____

2. Could Ott do a lot of genie tricks? _____

3. Was Ott the best of those in genie school? _____

4. What did Ott make when the teacher told him to make an apple?

   _____
       an alligator   an apple   a ship   a genie

5. What did Ott make when the teacher told him to make gold?

   a pot of b_____

6. Who ran into the school? _____
       a child   a teacher   an old woman   a yellow bottle

7. Who would have to go to the yellow bottle?

   one of the _____
       old genies   teachers   children from school

★★

1. What did the monster turn the king into? _____

2. The monster had a rod made of _____ .

3. The monster made Boo part _____ and part ghost.

> Three mean ghosts went to the farm.

1. Circle the words that tell who went to the farm.
2. Make a box around the word <u>went</u>.
3. Make a line over the words that tell where the ghosts went.

An elephant lived with jumping bugs. That elephant never saw another elephant. All she saw was bugs. So the elephant tried to be a bug. She tried to jump like a bug. But every time she jumped she made a hole in the ground. The bugs were getting mad at her. They kept saying, "You are not a bug. Stop trying to jump around."

One day the elephant met five other elephants. Now the elephant doesn't jump like a jumping bug. She walks like the other elephants.

1. Who did the elephant live with? _____

2. What did the elephant make when she jumped?

   _____ in the ground

3. Who said, "Stop trying to jump around"? _____

4. Does the elephant jump like a jumping bug now? _____

If a hat is spotted, it is old.

Circle every hat that is old.

NAME _____ TAKE-HOME **137** SIDE **1**

1. What is the name of the genie in this story? _____

2. Who said, "No, no. These children cannot go to work as genies"?

   _____

3. Who said, "I will give the children a test"? _____

4. The old woman said, "Make a _____ appear on the floor."

5. Did Ott make a peach or a beach? a _____

6. Which genie was sent to the yellow bottle? _____

7. What is the title of this story?

   _____

★★

1. How many ghosts lived with Boo? _____

2. Could any of those ghosts read? _____

3. Which ghost could read the words on the magic rod? _____

> The con fox ran fast.

1. Make a box around the word <u>ran</u>.

2. Circle the word that tells how he ran.

3. Make a line under the words that tell who ran fast.

Copyright © 1995 SRA Macmillan/McGraw-Hill. All rights reserved.

One day Boo was walking down the street. Boo had his magic rod. The monster jumped out and tried to take the rod from Boo. Boo held onto the rod and said, "Bid bide sap sape."

And what do you think happened to the monster? She turned into a teacher. She smiled. She was nice. She was smart. She was one of the best teachers you have ever seen.

1. What was Boo holding? the magic _____

2. Who wanted to take the rod from Boo? _____

3. Who said magic words? _____

4. What did the monster turn into? _____

| If a dog eats grass, she is sick. |

Circle every dog that is sick.

NAME _____   TAKE-HOME **138** SIDE **1**

1. What is the name of the genie in this story? _____

2. Was that genie very good at genie tricks? _____

3. What was the name of the girl who found the yellow bottle? _____

4. What street was she on? _____

5. How many boys began to follow Carla? _____

6. Did the boys think there was a genie in the bottle? _____

7. Did Carla really think there was a genie in the bottle? _____

8. Who came out of the bottle when Carla rubbed it? _____

★★★

| Fill in the blanks. |

1. When Ott tried to make a sound that was loud, he made a c_____ .

2. When Ott called for help, a _____ hit him in the face.

3. Carla tossed a bottle through a _____ .

> Pam tossed the ball over the hill.

1. Make a box around the word <u>tossed</u>.

2. Circle the word that tells who tossed the ball.

3. Make a line under the words that tell where she tossed the ball.

Once there was a bit of ice in an icebox. "It is cold in this icebox," the bit of ice said. "I will go where it is hot."

"If you go where it is hot you will melt," the other bits of ice said. But the bit of ice went to where it was hot. It wasn't long before she saw that she was getting smaller.

"I'm melting," the bit of ice said. "I must go back in the icebox." And she did. Now she is smaller but happy.

1. This story is about a bit of _____ .

2. The ice lived in an ice_____ .

3. Where did the ice want to go? where it is _____

4. What happened to the ice? She began to _____ .

5. Where is the bit of ice now? in the _____

If a tree is bent, it is old.

Circle every tree that is old.

NAME _____   TAKE-HOME **139** SIDE **1**

1. Who said, "Oh, master Carla, what can I do for you"? _____

2. Who said, "Give those boys a spanking"? _____

3. Did Ott give the boys a spanking or a banking? a _____

4. Ott told Carla that he was a very _____ genie.

5. Was that a lie? _____

6. Did Ott send Carla back home or to Rome? _____

7. What is the title of this story?

   _____

★★

1. What did the tiger have in his pouch? _____
       cash   stones   rocks   tigers

2. What did he get from the man at the stand?

   _____

3. He made the cone into a _____ .

> The genie looked small.

1. Make a w over the word looked.

2. Circle the word that tells how the genie looked.

3. Make a line under the words that tell what looked small.

A mean man had a bottle with a genie in it. Every day the mean man made the genie do tricks. But the mean man never liked the tricks. One day the mean man said, "I am tired of seeing you make gold appear. Let's see your best trick."

"Yes, master," the genie said. "I will show you my very best trick."

The genie waved his hands and turned the mean man into a log.

1. Who had the bottle? _____

2. Did the mean man like the genie's tricks? _____

3. Who said, "I will show you my very best trick"? _____

4. What did the man turn into? _____

| If a man is tired, he is sitting. |

Circle every man that is tired.

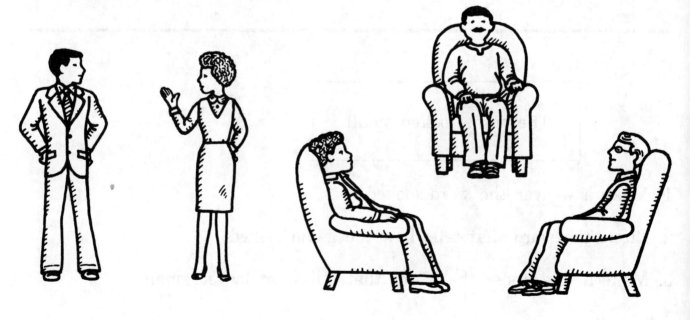

NAME _____ TAKE-HOME **140** SIDE **1**

1. What is the title of this story?

   _____

2. Where did Ott send Carla from the bank? to _____
       a spanking   her home   Rome   genie school

3. Where did they go from Rome? to _____
       Carla's home   a forest   a lake   a bank

4. Did Ott make an alligator or an apple? an _____

5. Did Ott make a peach or a beach? a _____

6. Who said, "You are a mess of a genie"? _____

7. Did Ott make a hot log or a hot dog? a _____

8. Was Ott happy or sad? _____

★★

1. What did the ghosts get from the monster? _____

2. Did they scare the monster? _____

3. Who turned the mean ghosts into happy ghosts? _____

> That pile of gold feels cold.

1. Make a box around the words that tell what feels cold.
2. Make a p over the word <u>feels.</u>
3. Circle the word that tells how the pile of gold feels.

Copyright © 1995 SRA Macmillan/McGraw-Hill. All rights reserved.

One day Spot met Boo the ghost. Boo had a magic rod. Spot said, "I want some bones. What do I say to make bones appear?"

Boo told Spot to hold the rod and say, "Hope, bone, bone, hope."

Spot tried to say that. But what she said was, "Home, cone, cone, home." When Spot said those words, she saw that she could fly like a bird. Now she has fun flying.

1. Who did Spot meet? _____

2. What did Boo have? a magic _____

3. What did Spot want? _____

4. Spot said, "Home, cone, _____ , _____ ."

5. Did Spot make bones appear? _____

Every fat bird likes bugs.

Circle every bird that likes bugs.

NAME _____   TAKE-HOME **141** SIDE **1**

1. Ott said, "I will make a sound that is very _____."

2. Did Ott make a sound that was loud? _____

3. What did he make? a _____

4. When Ott tried to make a cloud, he made a _____ sound.

5. Who gave Ott a kiss? _____

6. When Ott wished them to go to Rome, where did they go? _____

7. Who said, "I don't know how I do that"? _____

8. What is the title of this story?

_____

★★

| Fill in the blanks. |

1. Did Ott give the mean boys a spanking? _____

2. What did he give them? _____

3. Did Ott send Carla to her home or to Rome? _____

| This elephant sounds loud. |

1. Circle the word that tells how the elephant sounds.

2. Make a line under the word sounds.

3. Make a box around the words that tell what sounds loud.

Copyright © 1995 SRA Macmillan/McGraw-Hill. All rights reserved.

There was an alligator that liked to eat things. She ate a tiger. She ate a monster. She ate anything that got in her way. Ten bugs got in her way. She ate them. They tickled inside the alligator. When the alligator opened her mouth to laugh, all the animals came out. The tiger, the monster, and the ten bugs all came out. Now everybody is happy but the alligator.

1. What did the alligator like to do? _____

2. Who tickled her? _____

3. Did the bugs come out? _____

4. Did the monster come out? _____

5. Is the alligator happy now? _____

| Every white box is made of wood. |

Circle all the wood boxes.

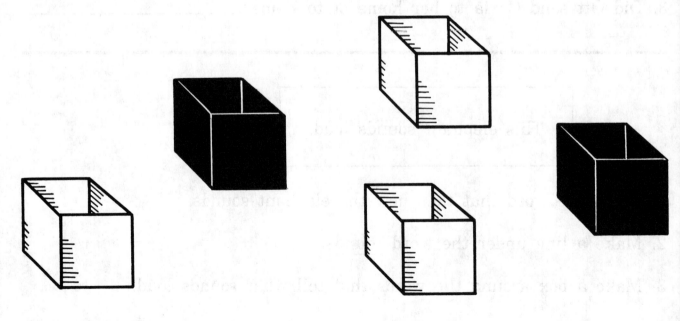

NAME _____   TAKE-HOME **142** SIDE **1**

1. What was streaming down Carla's cheek? a _____

2. Where were Ott and Carla? in _____

3. Did Ott tell Carla that he had lied to her? _____

4. Who tried to call for help? _____

5. What hit Ott in the face? a _____
      dish   fish   hot dog   beach

6. Who said, "I wish you would get out of here"? _____

7. Where did the bottle go
when Carla tossed it? _____
     crash   through a window   on the ground   fast

★★

1. Who began to howl when the
ghosts got near the castle? _____
     the monster   the hounds   the horse

2. Who was sitting at the table
when the ghosts floated in? _____
     Boo   the monster   the boss

3. Which ghost could read what it said on the magic rod? _____

> A car rolled down the hill.

1. Make a b over the word down.
2. Make a line under the words that tell where the car rolled.
3. Make a line over the words that tell what rolled down the hill.

A girl had six apples. These apples were in her house. The con fox had a plan for getting the apples. He made a big swing near the house. He got on the swing and began to swing very hard. Then he let go and went flying into the girl's house. But he landed in a tub. The girl picked him up and said, "What are you doing in here? You're all wet." So she put him on the line to dry. That con fox is not happy.

1. Who made a swing? _____
2. What was the fox trying to get? _____
3. What did he land in? _____
4. Who hung him on the line? _____
5. Why did she put the fox on the line? _____

| All the old coats are Bob's. |

Circle every coat that is Bob's.

NAME _____   TAKE-HOME **143** SIDE 1

1. Who went back into the yellow bottle? _____

2. Who came running from the house? _____
       a woman   Ott   a man   Carla

3. The woman said that _____ tossed the bottle through the window.
       Ott   an old genie   Carla

4. Who was going to spank Carla? _____

5. Who rubbed the bottle? _____

6. Ott fixed the _____ of glass in the window.
       pan   pane   pine   pin

7. Who said, "Please don't hate me"? _____

★★★

1. Don wanted to be a _____ man.

2. Where did Don work? in a _____ shop

3. When Don turned into a super man, he had a _____ and a _____ .

> The girls were mad.

1. Circle the words that tell who were mad.

2. Make a box around the word <u>were</u>.

3. Make a box around the word that tells how the girls felt.

Copyright © 1995 SRA Macmillan/McGraw-Hill. All rights reserved.

There was a fat cloud. That cloud was so fat that it could not keep up with the other clouds. The fat cloud became very sad and started to cry. When it cried, big drops of rain fell from the cloud. The cloud got smaller and smaller. Soon the cloud was not fat any more. Now the cloud can keep up with the other clouds.

1. The cloud was _____ .

2. Is the cloud fat now? _____

3. Why did the cloud cry? because it could not _____ _____ with the other clouds

4. When the cloud cried, it got s_____ .

| Every girl can read well. |

Circle every child who can read well.

NAME _____   TAKE-HOME **144** SIDE **1**

1. What is the title of this story?

   _____

2. Where were Ott and Carla? in _____

3. What did Ott get when he called for help? a _____
       hot dog   pane   peach   fish

4. Carla and Ott went to the park and sat in the _____ .
       shad   shade   home   stone

5. Carla found part of the book that said, "How to go _____ ."
       Rome   bone   home   stone

6. Who began to read the book out loud? _____

★★

1. Who scared the monster from the castle?

   the mean _____

2. The monster made Boo have a fish tail and a _____ .

3. The monster had turned the king into a _____ .

> The ball rolled down the hill.

1. Circle the words that tell what rolled down the hill.
2. Make a y over the word rolled.
3. Make a line under the words that tell where the ball rolled.

Jill was a horse with big, big feet. The other horses laughed at Jill. "Ho, ho," they said. "How can you run with those big feet?"
Then it began to rain a lot. The ground became mud. One horse tried to run in the mud but he got stuck. Another horse got stuck. So did another horse. Then Jill ran in the mud. But she did not get stuck. Her feet were too big to get stuck in the mud. The other horses said, "I wish I had big feet." Jill was happy.

1. What did Jill have? _____

2. Did the other horses get stuck in the mud? _____

3. Did Jill get stuck in the mud? _____

4. Who said, "I wish I had big feet"?

_____

Every small window has glass in it.

Circle every window with glass in it.

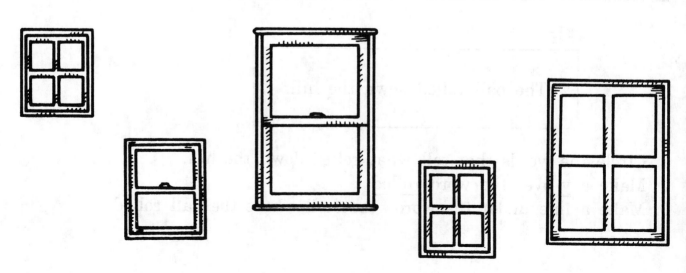

NAME _____   TAKE-HOME **145** SIDE 1

Make a line under the answer.

1. Carla was _____ from Ott's school book.
        reading   sitting   laughing

Fill in the blanks.

2. Carla said, "Ib, bub, ib, bub, ib, bub, bibby. Bome, _____,

_____ . I want to go _____ , _____ ,

_____ ."

3. Who said, "That is too much to remember"? _____

Circle the answer.

4. Who sent Carla home?
        an old genie   Carla   Ott

Fill in the blanks.

5. Did Ott go to Carla's home? _____

6. Who said, "I better call for help"? _____

★★

Fill in the blanks.

1. Who ran around and made a hole in the school? _____

2. What stopped in front of the school? _____
        a bus   a truck   a tree

3. Who was in the truck? a little _____

4. Who said, "You are too small for this job"? _____

If a cup has spots, it is hot.

Circle every cup that is hot.

There was a king who was very rich. So he had everything made out of gold. He had gold tables. He had gold lamps. He even had a gold bed. One day it got very cold out, so he put on his gold hat. Then he put on his gold boots and his gold pants. But he had so much gold on that he could not walk. He is still standing there in his gold things.

Fill in the blanks.

1. The king was very _____ .

2. What were his things made of? _____

3. Who put on a gold hat? _____

4. Could the king walk with all those gold things on? _____

NAME _____ TAKE-HOME **146** SIDE **1**

Circle the answer.

1. Carla was reading the part of the book that told how to call for _____ .
         home   hounds   horses   help

Fill in the blanks.

2. What is the title of this story?

_____

3. Did a fish drop from the sky when Carla called for help? _____

4. Did the old genie believe that Carla had called for help? _____

5. What did the old genie hold on her head? a _____
         rod   rock   rag   Ron

6. Did Carla turn it into water? _____

Make a line under the answer.

7. Who got mad?
         Ott   the old genie   Carla

Fill in the blanks.

8. Who said, "I need your help"? _____

9. Who did Carla want to find? _____

★★★

Fill in the blanks.

1. How many ghosts lived with Boo? _____

2. Were they nice to Boo? _____

3. Who said, "I have found somebody you can't scare"? _____

> If a boy has a hat on, he is cold.

Make a box around every boy who is cold.

Edna was an old lady who could not laugh. Her brother took her to funny shows. But she did not laugh. Then one day, she met a bug. The bug said, "My friends and I can make you laugh."

"No, you can't," Edna said. "Nothing can make me laugh."

So one hundred bugs came over. Ninety bugs sat on the old lady. And ten bugs tickled her and tickled her. She laughed and laughed and laughed.

> Circle the answers.

1. What couldn't the old lady do?   go to shows   sit   laugh

2. Who took her to shows?   her mother   her brother   her bugs

> Fill in the blanks.

3. Who said, "My friends and I can make you laugh"? _____

4. Who said, "No, you can't"? _____

5. Did the bugs make her laugh? _____

NAME _____   TAKE-HOME **147** SIDE **1**

Fill in the blanks.

1. What is the title of this story? _____

2. Did the old genie say that humans can't do very simple tricks? _____

Circle the answers.

3. Who said, "I will try to send another genie"?
       the old genie   Carla   Ott

4. Who was she talking to?   Carla   Ott   the teacher

Fill in the blank.

5. Who said, "I don't want another genie"? _____

Make a line over the answers.

6. Which genie did Carla want?
       the old genie   Ott   the teacher

7. Did the old genie let Carla go to genie school?
       Yes   No

If a boy is hungry, he is jumping.

Make a box around every boy who is hungry.

Copyright © 1995 SRA Macmillan/McGraw-Hill. All rights reserved.

Fill in the blanks.

1. One note from the boss said, "T_____ the oak tree near the door."

2. Another note said, "Send a c_____ to Sam's tree farm."

3. Another note said, "Plant seeds on the s_____."

Viz was a very sad window. He said, "Nobody looks at me. When people are on one side of me, they look at things that are on the other side of me. But they never look at me."

Then one night things got very cold. Ice formed on Viz, the window. The next day everybody said, "Look at the pretty window." Viz was a proud window now.

Fill in the blanks.

1. Who was sad? _____

2. Why was Viz sad? because nobody looked at _____

Make a line over the answer.

3. What happened one night?
    Things got cold.   Things got wet.   Things got hot.

Fill in the blanks.

4. What formed on that window? _____

5. Did people look at Viz the next day? _____

Every rat thinks.   Linda is a rat.

What does Linda do? _____

NAME _____   TAKE-HOME **148** SIDE 1

Fill in the blanks.

1. What is the title of this story?

   _____

2. When Carla snapped her fingers, a _____ appeared.

3. She told the boy to _____ on the rock.

Make a line over the answers.

4. Then she turned the rock into _____ .

       a bottle   water   a genie

5. Who was the best at doing tricks?

       Ott   Carla   a little genie

6. Soon it was time for the children to take their genie _____ .

       now   how   vow   cow

If the dog is little, he can run fast.

Make a line under every dog that can run fast.

Copyright © 1995 SRA Macmillan/McGraw-Hill. All rights reserved.

Fill in the blanks.

1. A tame tiger liked ice c_____ .

2. Did the tiger have cash? _____

3. Did the tiger want a con or a cone? _____

A little girl was mad because she was so small. She said, "I wish I was big. I wish I was bigger than anybody."

Boo was hiding near the girl. He took the magic rod and said some magic words. The girl began to grow bigger and bigger. Soon she was as big as a house. Then she began to cry. She said, "I don't like to be so big. I wish I was small again." So Boo made her small again. Now she is happy.

Fill in the blanks.

1. Why was the girl sad? because she was so _____

2. Who said, "I wish I was big"? _____

3. Who made her get bigger and bigger? _____

4. Was the girl happy when she was big? _____

5. She said, "I _____ I was small again."

Every dog pants.   Rob is a dog.

What does Rob do? _____

NAME _____   TAKE-HOME **149** SIDE **1**

Make a line under the answers.

1. Who told the children about what a genie had to do?
    Ott   Carla   the old genie

2. Who began to cry?
    Ott   Carla   the old genie

3. Was Carla ready to forget about herself
   and do what her master told her?   Yes   No

Fill in the blanks.

4. Was the old genie mad at her? _____

5. Were the other children mad at Carla? _____

6. What is the title of this story?

_____

7. Did Carla take the genie vow? _____

All of the short boys have dogs.

Make a box around every boy who has a dog.

Fill in the blanks.

1. What did Ott make when he tried to make a hot dog? _____

2. What did Ott make when he tried to make an apple? _____

3. What did Ott make when he tried to make a peach? _____

There was a genie named Itt. She could not do many genie tricks. One day she tried to make a truck appear. But she made a trunk appear. Then she tried to make a hot dog. But she made a hot frog. That frog was mad. He hopped in the pond to cool off.

Fill in the blanks.

1. What was the genie's name? _____

2. What couldn't she do? many genie _____

3. What did she make for a truck? _____

4. What did she make for a hot dog? _____

Every car has doors.   Sid has a car.

What does Sid's car have? _____

NAME _____   TAKE-HOME 150 SIDE 1

Fill in the blanks.

1. What is the title of this story? _____

2. Which genie went to a yellow bottle that belonged to Carla? _____

3. Was Ott happy? _____

Make a box around the answers.

4. Who told the old genie that some new bottles had been found?
       Ott   the teacher   Carla

5. How many bottles were found?   six   five   three

Fill in the blanks.

6. Who is training genies at the school now?

   _____ and _____

7. Is Ott a good teacher? _____

8. Carla is a good teacher because she is very _____ .

9. Is there more to come in this story? _____

All the girls with long hair have pets.

Make a line over the girls who have pets.

Copyright © 1995 SRA Macmillan/McGraw-Hill. All rights reserved.

TAKE-HOME 150 SIDE 2

Fill in the blanks.

1. What did Ott make when he tried to make an apple? _____

2. What did Ott make when he tried to make a peach? _____

3. Who told Ott that he would have to go into the yellow bottle? the old g_____

Once there was a sad horse. The horse had flies on her back. She tried to get rid of the flies but she couldn't. The flies kept biting her and biting her.
At last the horse yelled, "I hate flies."
A bird said, "I don't hate them. I love them."
The bird hopped on the horse's back and ate the flies. Now the horse is happy and so is the bird.

Fill in the blank.

1. What did the horse have on her back? _____

Circle the answer.

2. Could the horse get rid of the flies?
　　　Yes　　No

Make a box under the answers.

3. Who loved flies?
　　　the bird　　the farmer　　the horse

4. The bird _____ the flies.　　kissed　　ate　　hugged

Every bird eats bugs.　　Ron is a bird.

What does Ron do? _____

Printed in the United States of America.

NAME _____   TAKE-HOME **151** SIDE **1**

> Fill in the blanks.

1. What is the title of this story?
   _____

2. Who grabbed a fly and ate it? _____

> Make a box around the answer.

3. Who jumped way up?

       a turtle   a snake   a frog

> Fill in the blanks.

4. Did the turtle jump way up? _____

5. Was the frog nice to the turtle? _____

> Circle the answer.

6. Did the turtle feel happy or sad?

       happy   sad

> Every big box has kittens in it.

Circle every box with kittens in it.

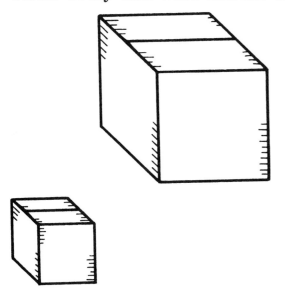

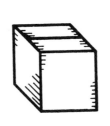
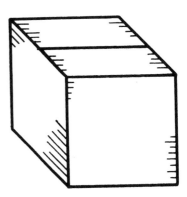

Copyright © 1995 SRA Macmillan/McGraw-Hill. All rights reserved.

TAKE-HOME 151 SIDE 2

Fill in the blanks.

1. Who planted seeds in the slop? _____

2. Who told Sid, "I will teach you to read"? _____

3. Did the boss teach Sid to read well? _____

A weed is a plant that people don't want. In some parts of the world, a rose is called a weed. We think a rose is a pretty flower. But it is a weed when it grows where nobody wants it. And we like some plants that grow like weeds in other parts of the world.

Fill in the blanks.

1. A weed is a _____ that people don't _____ .

2. Could a pretty flower be a weed? _____

3. Could a big plant be a weed? _____

4. A plant that you buy is not a _____ .

5. Could a rose be a weed? _____

Every house has windows.   I made a house.

What do you know about the house I made?

_____

NAME _____   TAKE-HOME **152** SIDE **1**

> Circle the answers.

1. What was Flame?

    a woman   a snake   a frog

2. Could the turtle do things the frog could do?

    Yes   No

> Fill in the blanks.

3. What is the title of this story?

   _____

4. Who told the turtle that he looked like a toenail? _____

> Make a line under the answer.

5. Who was looking for frogs?

    a turtle   a snake   a frog

> Fill in the blank.

6. Did the turtle tell a lie to the snake? _____

> Jane will buy every bottle that is little and round.

Circle every bottle that Jane will buy.

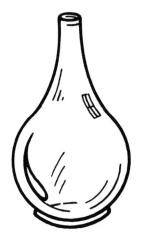    

TAKE-HOME 152 SIDE 2

Fill in the blanks.

1. Did Ott give the mean boys a spanking or a banking? _____

2. What did Ott make when he tried to make a hot dog? _____

3. Where did Ott send Carla when he tried to send her home? _____

Some caves are holes under the ground. Some caves are small and some are big. Small animals like to sleep in caves that are on the side of mountains. Some caves are very big. In one big cave you could walk for over 80 miles. You could walk for days and days and not see every part of the cave. And you would never see the sun while you were in that cave. The cave is under the ground and things are very dark there.

Fill in the blanks.

1. Some caves are big _____ under the _____ .

2. Are all caves big? _____

3. If you were in a big cave would you see the sun? _____

4. In one big cave you could walk for over _____ miles.

5. In that cave, you could walk for _____ and _____ .

Every bottle is made of glass.   I have a bottle.

What do you know about the bottle I have?

_____

Printed in the United States of America.

NAME _____   TAKE-HOME **153** SIDE **1**

> Circle the answer.

1. Did the turtle lie to the snake?   Yes   No

> Fill in the blanks.

2. What's the title of this story? _____
_____

3. Was Flame fast? _____

4. Was Flame a sneak? _____

> Make a box around the answers.

5. Where did the frog jump when Flame was chasing him?

    into the weeds   into the pond   into a tree

6. Who said, "I'll bite you on the nose"?

    the frog   the snake   the turtle

> Fill in the blank.

7. Did the snake try to bite the turtle? _____

> Every dog with long ears is named Sandy.

Circle every dog named Sandy.

Copyright © 1995 SRA Macmillan/McGraw-Hill. All rights reserved.

Fill in the blanks.

1. The old genie told the teacher that a girl had found a _____.

2. Did the teacher think that Ott should go to the bottle? _____

3. What did Ott make when he tried to make a loud sound? _____

Trees have roots. The roots are under the ground. The roots hold the tree up and keep it from falling over. The roots also carry water from the ground to the tree. So the roots do two things. They hold the tree up and they bring water to the tree. Trees could not live if they did not have roots.

Fill in the blanks.

1. All trees have _____ .

2. Where are the roots? under the _____

3. How many things do the roots do? _____

4. They keep the tree from _____ over.

5. They bring _____ to the tree.

6. Could trees live if they didn't have roots? _____

Every girl has a short dress.   Terry is a girl.

What do you know about her? _____

NAME _____ TAKE-HOME **154** SIDE **1**

> Fill in the blanks.

1. What is the title of this story? _____
_____

2. Did Flame try to bite the turtle? _____

> Make a line under the answers.

3. Flame hit her tooth on the turtle's _____ .

      nose   shell   ear

4. Flame said, "I think I broke my _____ ."

      nose   shell   tooth

> Fill in the blanks.

5. Did the turtle let Flame go after the frog? _____

6. Was the turtle happy? _____

> Ann has all the dogs with spots.

Circle every dog that Ann has.

Copyright © 1995 SRA Macmillan/McGraw-Hill. All rights reserved.

TAKE-HOME 154 SIDE 2

Fill in the blanks.

1. Who told Don to come down the stairs? _____

2. Don became a super man when he _____ the dime.

3. What did Don give to the little man? _____

Some caves are big holes under the ground. Animals live in some of the big caves. These animals are fish and bugs. They spend all their time in the dark. They never see the sun. And they are very strange. Most of them are white. They cannot see because they never have to use their eyes. Remember the two ways that they are strange: they cannot see, and they are white.

Fill in the blanks.

1. The animals that live in big caves are _____ and _____.

2. What color are most of these animals? _____

3. Can these animals see? _____

4. These animals never see the _____.

5. Is it light or dark in the big caves? _____

6. So do these animals need eyes that see? _____

All kites are red.   Mom has a kite.

What do you know about her kite? _____

NAME _____   TAKE-HOME **155** SIDE **1**

> Make a line over the answers.

1. Who slid into the weeds?

    the turtle   the snake   the frog

2. Who bit the snake?

    the turtle   the snake   the frog

> Fill in the blanks.

3. Where did the frog hide? _____

4. Could he jump well in the weeds? _____

> Circle the answers.

5. Did the frog come out of the weeds?   Yes   No

6. Does Flame go after the frog any more? Yes   No

> Ted made every coat that is white.

Circle every coat that Ted made.

TAKE-HOME 155 SIDE 2

Fill in the blanks.

1. Flame hit her tooth on the turtle's _____

2. Did the turtle let Flame go after the frog? _____

3. Could the frog jump well in the weeds? _____

Once there was a frog that liked to stick to things. One day, the frog said, "I will stick to this log." But the frog did not stick to a log. The frog stuck to an alligator's nose.

The alligator said, "I will open my mouth and the frog will fall in." The alligator opened her mouth. The frog did not fall in. The frog just stuck to the alligator's nose.

The frog said, "I like this log. It goes up and down. I will stick here all day." And he did.

Fill in the blanks.

1. Who liked to stick to things? _____

2. Did the frog stick to a log? _____

3. He stuck to an alligator's _____ .

Circle the answers.

4. Who opened her mouth?   a frog   an alligator   a log

5. Did the frog like to stick on the alligator's nose?   Yes   No

Fill in the blanks.

6. The alligator's nose went _____ and _____ .

All rabbits hop.   Al has a rabbit.

What does Al's rabbit do? _____

Printed in the United States of America.

TAKE-HOME 156 SIDE 1

Fill in the blanks.

1. What is the title of this story? _____

_____

2. Who said, "Sleep hard"? _____

Circle the answers.

3. Did Jean sleep hard?   Yes   No

4. Who did Jean meet?   a dog   a wizard   a lady

Fill in the blanks.

5. The wizard told her, "All _____ are mean."

6. Did Jean see strange animals? _____

Make a line over the answer.

7. The name of the land in Jean's dream was the land of _____.

   peevish pets   many pits   peevish pits

Circle the right rule.

8. All crumps are mean.   All little drumps are mean.

   Some little crumps are mean.   All little crumps are mean.

Every boy with a coat and a hat is hungry.

Circle every boy who is hungry.

TAKE-HOME 156 SIDE 2

Fill in the blanks.

1. Carla told the old genie to hold a _____ on her head.

2. Did the old genie get wet? _____

3. Did Carla take her genie vow? _____

    If you jumped from a ladder, you would go down. If you jumped from a plane, you would fall down. But if you were very, very far from the ground, things would not be the same. When you are very, very far from the ground, you are in space. Things don't fall in space. If you stepped from a ladder in space, you would float. You would not go down. Things do not fall in space. So there is no up or down in space.

Fill in the blanks.

1. When you are very, very far from the ground, you are in _____.

2. Do things fall when you are near the ground? _____

3. Do things fall when you are in space? _____

4. If you stepped from a ladder in space, you would _____.

5. There is no _____ or _____ in space.

All mips are green.   Mom has a mip.

What do you know about her mip? _____

Printed in the United States of America.

NAME _____ TAKE-HOME **157** SIDE **1**

Fill in the blanks.

1. What was the name of the land Jean was in? the land of _____

2. What kind of crumps are mean? _____

3. Who told Jean how to make the mean crumps go away? _____

4. How many rules did Jean have to know before she could go home? _____

Make a line over the answers.

5. What did Jean say to make the crumps go away?

   "Away."   "Go away, away."   "Away, away."   "Get out of here."

6. Did the mean crump go away when Jean said that?
         Yes   No

Fill in the blank.

7. What is the title of this story?

_____

If it has spots and two ears, it is a glim.

Circle every glim.

TAKE-HOME 157 SIDE 2

Fill in the blanks.

1. Ott went to a school for _____.

2. Carla found a yellow _____.

3. How many teachers are now teaching in the genie school? _____

4. What are their names? _____

Once there was a hound that was very tired. The hound did not have a place to sleep. And the night was cold and wet. so the hound began to howl. "Owww," she said.

She woke the people up. They got mad. They tossed socks, hats, shoes, and coats at the hound. They tossed things until there was a big pile of stuff.

Then the dog said, "Now I have a place to sleep." So the dog went to sleep in the pile of socks, hats, shoes, and coats.

Make a box around the answer.

1. The hound was very _____.   happy   fast   old   tired

Make a line under the answer.

2. But she did not have a place to _____.   eat   hide   sleep

Fill in the blanks.

3. So she began to _____.

4. Then the dog said, "Now I have a _____ to _____."

All mip food is in a can.   Dan has mip food.

What do you know about Dan's mip food? _____

NAME _____   TAKE-HOME **158** SIDE **1**

Fill in the blanks.

1. All _____ crumps are _____.

2. Jean was in the land of _____ _____.

3. How many rules did Jean have to know before she could go home? _____

4. What did she say to make mean crumps go away? _____

5. Every dusty path leads _____.

Circle the answers.

6. Who told Jean the rule about the dusty paths?

    a wizard   a crump   her mother

7. The water in the lake was _____.

    pink   red   deep

Fill in the blanks.

8. Could Jean get away from the lake by taking a dusty path? _____

9. Why not? _____

_____

Find out where the bugs are.

Here is the rule: Every white house has bugs.

    Kim's house is brown.
    Spot's house is white.
    Ott's house is white.
    Tim's house is red.
    Mom's house is black.

Who has a house with bugs? _____ _____

Copyright © 1995 SRA Macmillan/McGraw-Hill. All rights reserved.

TAKE-HOME 158 SIDE 2

> All feps are words.

Carmen has feps.

What do you know about Carmen's feps? _____

There was a bug who couldn't run. "I will teach you to run," a wolf said. "Move your legs very fast."

The bug tried it. "No," the wolf said. "You are dancing, not running. Move up and down."

The bug tried. "No," the wolf said. "You are hopping."

The wolf showed her teeth. The bug got scared and ran faster than any bug you have ever seen.

> Fill in the blanks.

1. The _____ said, "I will teach you to _____."

> Make a circle over the answer.

2. First the wolf told the bug to move his legs _____.

    up and down   here and there   very fast

> Make a box under the answer.

3. Then the wolf told the bug to move _____.

    up and down   here and there   very fast

> Fill in the blanks.

4. The _____ got scared and _____

faster than any _____ you have ever seen.

NAME _____   TAKE-HOME 159 SIDE 1

Make a line under the answers.

1. The dusty paths led right back _____.

    to the mountain   to the lake   to a cake

2. Before Jean could leave the land of peevish pets, she had to know _____.

    sixteen rules   one more rule   twenty rules

Fill in the blanks.

3. The wizard told her that every rocky path leads _____.

4. What did Jean see all around the mountain? _____

5. Who ran after Jean? _____

6. What did Jean say to make the mean crumps go away? _____

Find out who will go to Japan.

| Here is the rule: The people who are running will go to Japan. |

　　　The boss is running.
　　　Ellen is running.
　　　Boo is sitting.
　　　Jean is standing.
　　　The turtle is not running.

Who will go to Japan? _____ _____

> All glicks are small.   Ann has a glick.

What do you know about her glick? _____

      There was a dog that said, "I hate to take a bath."
That dog had bugs. The dog said, "I hate bugs."
      One day a woman said, "That dog has bugs, so I will give the dog a bath."
      The dog said, "I hate baths."
      His bugs said, "We hate baths, too."
      The woman gave the dog a bath, and the bugs went away.
Now the dog says, "I like baths. They made my bugs go away."

> Fill in the blanks.

1. Did the dog like baths or hate baths? _____ baths

2. Who said, "We hate baths, too"? _____

3. Who said, "I will give the dog a bath"? _____

4. Why does the dog like baths now?

   _____

NAME _____   TAKE-HOME **160** SIDE **1**

Fill in the blanks.

1. What is the title of this story?
   _____

2. Who told the rule about red food? _____

3. What is the rule about red food?
   _____

Make a line under the answers.

4. Did Jean eat the ice cream?   Yes   No
5. Did Jean eat the red banana?   Yes   No
6. Did Jean eat the white grapes?   Yes   No

Find out who has frogs.

Rule: There are frogs in every tin cup.

   Ellen has a tin cup.
   Ott does not have a tin cup.
   Sid has a tin cup.
   Spot does not have a tin cup.
   Boo has a tin cup.

Who has frogs? _____ _____ _____

All flying bats are mammals.   Fred is a flying bat.

What do you know about him? _____

   Some trees have very good wood. Other trees have wood that is not so good. The good wood is made into tables and chairs and other wooden things. Do you know what happens to the wood that is not so good? It is made into paper. The next time you use some paper, remember that you are using a tree.

Fill in the blank.

1. Do all trees have very good wood? _____

Circle the answers.

2. Good wood is made into _____.

   windows and streets   tables and chairs   paper

3. Wood that is not so good is made into _____.

   paper   tables and chairs   streets

Make a line under the answer.

4. What is the best title for this story?

   Some Trees Have Good Wood

   Tables and Chairs Are Made of Wood

   Paper Comes from Trees

NAME _____   TAKE-HOME **161** SIDE 1

Fill in the blanks.

1. What is the name of the land in Jean's dream? _____

2. How many rules did she have to know before she could leave? _____

3. What did Jean know about all little crumps? _____

4. What do you do to make a mean crump go away? _____

5. What kind of path goes to the lake? _____

6. What kind of path goes to the mountain? _____

7. What kind of food is good to eat? _____

8. What happened to Jean when she ate three red bananas?

   _____

9. Was Jean happy or sad? _____

Find out which girls are sitting on a pin.

Rule: Every girl who is crying is sitting on a pin.

   Ned is laughing.
   Peg is not crying.
   Pam is crying.
   Jane is playing ball.
   Linda is crying.

Which girls are sitting on a pin? _____   _____

Copyright © 1995 SRA Macmillan/McGraw-Hill. All rights reserved.

Every lion is sleepy.   Peg is a lion.

What do you know about her? _____

Did you know that glass melts? If you take a bottle and make it very hot, you can melt it. First, the bottle will become soft. When the bottle gets hotter and hotter, the glass will start to turn red. When the glass is very, very hot, it will flow like water. Watch out when glass melts. It is very, very hot.

Circle the answer.

1. The best title for this story is _____.

    Glass Melts   Glass Becomes Soft   A Bottle

Fill in the blanks.

2. If you make a bottle very hot, what happens first?

   It will become _____.

3. What color will the bottle become? _____

4. Then the glass will flow like _____.

5. Would you touch glass when it was melting? _____

Make a line under the answer.

6. Does glass melt?   Yes   No

NAME _____   TAKE-HOME **162** SIDE **1**

Fill in the blanks.

1. What's the title of this story? _____

   _____

2. What happened to Jean when she ate three red bananas? _____

   _____

3. Who told Jean how to make the stripes disappear? _____

4. "If you _____ in the lake, the stripes _____

   _____."

5. Which path did Jean take to the lake? _____

Find out who is going to the store.

Rule: If a boy is in the park, he is going to the store.

    Jack is in the school.
    Bob is in the park.
    Pam is in the house.
    Tom is in the park.
    Ted is in the bedroom.

Who is going to the store? _____ _____

Every cup has a handle.   I have a cup.

What do you know about the cup I have? _____

    A man named Isaac Newton lived a long time back. One day he was sitting under a tree. An apple dropped on his head. He began to think about that apple. He made up a rule about things. Here is his rule: "What goes up must come down."

Fill in the blanks.

1. Who was sitting under the tree? _____

2. What dropped on his head? _____

3. Newton made up a _____.

4. "What goes _____ must come _____."

NAME _____   TAKE-HOME **163** SIDE **1**

Fill in the blanks.

1. Why did Jean have red stripes? _____
   _____

2. What did she have to do to make the stripes disappear?
   _____

Circle the answers.

3. Which path did she take to the lake?

   the muddy path   the dusty path   the rocky path

4. How many little crumps were on the path?

   five   six   one   three

5. What did she say to make the crumps go away?

   "Away, you crumps."   "Away."   "Away, away."

Fill in the blanks.

6. Did the stripes disappear when she jumped into the lake? _____

7. What color was her hair now? _____

8. If you stand _____, the white hair will go away.

Find out who ate crackers.

| Rule: The people who ate crackers are sleeping. |

   Jane is playing ball.
   Jean is sleeping.
   Tim is sleeping.
   The boss is yelling at Sid.
   Ellen is sleeping.

Who ate crackers? _____ _____ _____

Copyright © 1995 SRA Macmillan/McGraw-Hill. All rights reserved.

| All weeds are plants. | Marta has a weed.

What do you know about Marta's weed? _____

Here is a rule about all living things: All living things grow, and all living things need water. Is a tree a living thing? Yes. So you know that a tree grows, and you know that a tree needs water. A dog is a living thing. So what do you know about a dog? You know a dog grows. You know that a dog needs water. You are a living thing. Do you grow? Yes. Do you need water? Yes.

| Fill in the blanks. |

1. All living things _____ .

2. All living things need _____ .

3. Is a fly a living thing? _____

4. Name two things you know about a fly. _____
   _____

5. Is a dog a living thing? _____

6. So you know that a dog _____ .

   And you know that a dog needs _____ .

7. Is a chair a living thing? _____

8. Does a chair need water? _____

NAME _____   TAKE-HOME **164** SIDE 1

Fill in the blanks.

1. What did Jean do to make the stripes disappear? _____

2. What color was her hair after she jumped in the lake? _____

3. What's the title of this story? _____
   _____

4. What did Jean do to make the white disappear? _____

Make a line under the answers.

5. Now Jean was _____ .

       big   bald   green   old

6. What did Jean have to do to get her hair back?

       clamp her hands   clap her hands   clamp her teeth

Find out who has cash.

Rule: Every red bottle has cash in it.

    Sandy has a red bottle.
    Tom has four yellow bottles.
    The boss has two red bottles.
    Mom has one red bottle.
    Spot has a red dish.

Who has cash? _____ _____ _____

TAKE-HOME **164** SIDE **2**

| All rits are little. | Sop is a rit.

What do you know about Sop? _____

    Remember the rule about living things: All living things grow, and all living things need water. Here is another rule about all living things. All living things make babies. A tree is a living thing. A tree makes baby trees. A fish is a living thing. A fish makes baby fish. A spider is a living thing. A spider makes baby spiders. Remember the rule: All living things make babies.

| Fill in all the blanks. |

1. What do all living things make? _____

2. Is a fish a living thing? _____

3. So a fish makes _____ _____.

4. Is a spider a living thing? _____

5. So a spider makes _____ _____.

6. Is a chair a living thing? _____

7. Does a chair make baby chairs? _____

8. Name two things you know about living things.

   All living things _____.

   All living things need _____.

NAME _____   TAKE-HOME **165** SIDE **1**

> Make a box around the answers.

1. Did Jean get her hair back?   Yes   No

2. What color was her hair?
       red   yellow   white

> Make a line under the answer.

3. A _____ animal came out of the lake.
       sitting   talking   smiling

> Fill in the blanks.

4. Did the animal tell Jean the right rule about dusty paths? _____

5. Did he tell Jean the right rule about jumping in the lake? _____

> Circle the answer.

6. What did he tell her to say so that she could have fun?
    "Side, slide."   "Slide, slide."   "Side, side."

Find out who likes monsters.

> Rule: Everybody who is smiling likes monsters.

    The boss is yelling at Jan.
    Jan is very sad.
    Ellen is smiling.
    The tiger is smiling.
    Dad has a tear in his eye.

Who likes monsters? _____ _____

Copyright © 1995 SRA Macmillan/McGraw-Hill. All rights reserved.

> All nails are made of metal.   Ann has a nail.

What do you know about her nail? _____

There once was a girl with a cold head. She said, "I need a warm hat." So she got a nice big hat. But the wind blew her hat away. The girl yelled, "My head is cold again." And she ran after her hat. She fell down in some mud. A big chunk of mud stuck to her head. The girl smiled and said, "Now my head is not cold. It is warm. This mud is better than a hat." The girl wore the mud hat for three years. Soon she had many plants growing from her hat.

> Make a box over the answer.

1. The girl had a _____ head.

   cold   fat   big   old

> Fill in the blanks.

2. She said, "I _____ a warm _____."

> Circle the answer.

3. She fell in some _____.

   plants   mud   water   flowers

> Fill in the blanks.

4. She wore the mud _____ for _____ years.

> Make a box over the answer.

5. What is growing from the hat now?

   trees   plants   bugs

NAME _____   TAKE-HOME **166** SIDE 1

Fill in the blanks.

1. Who told Jean what to say if
   she wanted to have fun? the _____ animal

2. He said, "If you want to have fun, say '_____.'"

3. Jean was up to her _____ in snow.

4. What do you say if you want to be cold? _____

5. What do you say if you
   want to be warm again? _____

Circle the answers.

6. Did the talking animal tell the right rule about dusty paths?

       Yes   No

7. Did he tell the right rule about having fun?

       Yes   No

8. Make up a rule about talking animals. Talking animals _____.

       do good things   lie   tell bedtime stories

Find out where the mice are.

Rule: Every big house has mice in it.

    The boss has a little house.
    Sid has a big house.
    Ann has a big horse.
    Jean has a big house.
    Sam's house is very big.

Who has a house with mice? _____ _____ _____

| All dogs sleep. | Mike is a dog.

What do you know about Mike? _____

 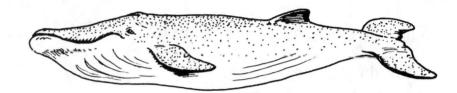

    Some animals are very small. And other animals are very big. A mouse is small. A bug is even smaller. There are animals smaller than a bug. The biggest animal that lives on land is the elephant. Every day he eats a pile of grass bigger than you are. But the elephant is not the biggest animal there is. The biggest animal is the whale. Whales do not live on land. Whales live in the sea. Some whales are bigger than ten elephants.

| Fill in the blanks. |

1. Is a mouse a big animal? _____

2. Name an animal that is smaller than a mouse. _____

3. Is a bug the smallest animal there is? _____

4. What is the biggest animal that lives on land? _____

5. Name an animal that is bigger than an elephant. _____

6. Where do whales live? _____

7. Some _____ are bigger than _____ elephants.

NAME _____

TAKE-HOME **167** SIDE **1**

Fill in the blanks.

1. What is the rule about how to be cold? _____

2. What do you say if you want to be warm again?

   _____

3. What is the rule about talking animals? Talking animals _____.

4. If a talking animal tells you that pink ice cream is good, you know that pink ice cream is _____.

Make a line over the answers.

5. Who did Jean meet? a talking _____

      bug   tree   lady

6. The bug said, "I never _____."

      eat   talk   sleep

Find out who has ice cream.

Rule: The animals that are taking a bath have ice cream.

The tiger is taking a bath.
The lion is walking with the mouse.
The cat is taking a bath.
The turtle is taking a bath.
The frog is sleeping on a log.

Who has ice cream?

_____ _____ _____

TAKE-HOME 167 SIDE 2

| All ticks have six legs. | I have a tick.

What do you know about my tick? _____

    Trees do not grow in the winter because the ground is cold. In the spring the sun begins to make the ground warmer and warmer. First the top of the ground gets warm. Then the deeper parts of the ground get warm. Every year small trees begin to grow before big trees grow. Small trees grow first because their roots are not very deep in the ground. So their roots warm up before the roots of big trees warm up.

| Fill in the blanks. |

1. When do trees begin to grow? in the _____

2. Trees do not grow in the _____.

3. Trees begin to grow when their roots get _____.

4. Why do small trees grow first every year? _____

_____

NAME _____

TAKE-HOME **168** SIDE **1**

> Fill in the blanks.

1. What is the title of this story? _____
_____

2. What do you say if you want to be cold? _____
_____

3. What is the rule about talking animals?
_____

4. What do you say if you want to be warm again?
_____

5. Jean told the bug to tell her about something that is really _____.

> Circle the answers.

6. What happened when Jean tapped her foot three times?
   She began to _____.

       sneak   snake   fly   cry

7. What did the strange man say to Jean?

       "Arf."   "Barn, barn."   "Bark, bark."

       "Hello, there."

Find out who is smart.

> Rule: The people with hats are smart.

    Kim has a hat.
    Sid has a hat.
    The boss does not have a hat.
    Ellen has a hat.
    Spot does not have a hat.

Who is smart? _____ _____ _____

All bikes have wheels.   Tom has a bike.

What do you know about Tom's bike? _____

Some mountains are miles tall. The tallest mountain in the U.S. is in Alaska. It is nearly four miles tall. But it is not the tallest mountain in the world. The tallest mountain in the world is named Everest. Everest is in a land called Tibet. Everest is over five miles tall.

Fill in the blanks.

1. The tallest mountain in the U.S. is in _____.

2. How many miles tall is that mountain? _____

3. The tallest mountain in the world is in a land called _____.

4. That mountain is named _____.

5. Everest is over _____ miles tall.

NAME _____   TAKE-HOME **169** SIDE **1**

Circle the answers.

1. Who did Jean trick? A talking _____
      cat   rat   bug   bat

2. What did Jean do so that she could fly?
      said, "side, slide"   tapped her foot three times

Fill in the blanks.

3. What is the rule about talking animals?
_____

4. What did the man hand Jean? _____

5. If you tell the man to become a dog, the man becomes _____.

6. Every time Jean says, "But what and when . . . ," the wizard
_____.

7. How many more rules did Jean need to leave the land of peevish pets? _____

Find out who has a bug.

| Rule: Every fat bottle has a bug in it. |

      Pat's bottle is fat.
      Fred's bottle is not fat.
      Don's bottle is fat.
      Ellen's bottle is not fat.
      Sandy's bottle is not fat.

Who has a bug? _____ _____

| All dops are made of wood. | I have a dop. |

What do you know about my dop? _____

___

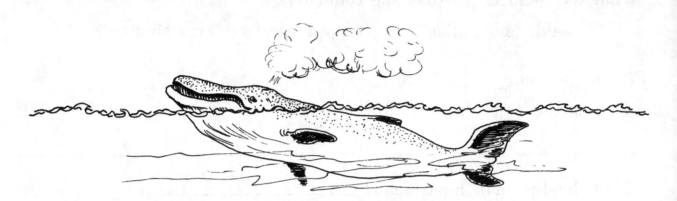

    Do you remember which land animal is the biggest? The elephant. Which is the biggest animal of all? The whale. Where does the whale live? In the sea. But a whale is not a fish. Here is the rule: Fish breathe water. Can you breathe water? No. Can a dog breathe water? No. Can a whale breathe water? No. Whales must breathe air, just like you and me. Whales have a hole at the top of their heads. They stick their heads out of the water and breathe air. Remember, a whale is not a fish.

| Fill in the blanks. |

1. Which land animal is the biggest? _____

2. Which animal is the biggest of all? _____

3. Where does the whale live? _____

4. Can you breathe water? _____

5. Can a whale breathe water? _____

6. A whale is _____ a _____ .

NAME _____ TAKE-HOME **170** SIDE **1**

Fill in the blanks.

1. How do you make the wizard appear?

    Say, "_____."

2. How do you make the wizard disappear?

    Say, "_____."

3. What was on Jean's bed? _____

4. What was the name of the puppy? _____

5. The note said, "If you love him and _____ with him, he

    will grow up to be the _____ dog in the _____."

6. Was Jean happy or sad? _____

Find out who is a boss.

Rule: Every boss has short hair.

    Tom has short hair.
    Carol has short hair.
    Ron has long hair.
    Ellen has no hair.
    Pam has short hair.

Who is a boss? _____ _____ _____

TAKE-HOME 170 SIDE 2

| All mups have red ears. | Ellen is a mup.

What do you know about Ellen? _____

    The first people lived thousands and thousands of years back. These people needed food, but they couldn't go to the store and buy food. There were no food stores. There were no stores of any kind. So these people had to hunt animals. But they did not have guns. They did not have arrows. So they had to use rocks and sticks to kill animals. But some animals were hard to kill. They were big and mean. The men would hide behind trees and jump out at the animal. Sometimes they would kill the animal. Sometimes the animal would get away. Sometimes the animal would kill them.

| Fill in the blanks.

1. The first people lived _____ and _____ of years back.

2. Could these people buy food at a store? _____

3. Did they have guns and arrows? _____

4. What did they use to kill animals? _____ and _____

5. Sometimes they would kill the animal. But sometimes the _____ would kill them.